"I WAS JUST A RADIOMAN"

The Memoirs of ARM H. P. Lawrence

Compiled by
Pamela Ackerson

"I WAS JUST A RADIOMAN"

Edited by Chrissy Szarek

Disclaimer:
This is a memoir about the real and true experiences of
Chief ARM H. P. Lawrence, a Pearl Harbor survivor, Black
Cat, and decorated World War II veteran.

The day that will live in infamy was just the beginning. This is the story of one man, Henry P. Lawrence, a Pearl Harbor survivor, Black Cat, and decorated war veteran.

1940

Let me tell you how this all came about...

In June of 1940, my brother, Frank, and I joined the Ninth Division, US Naval Reserve Unit at the State Armory on Thames Street in Newport, RI. All of our drills were held at the Armory on Wednesday evenings.

We were required to march in uniform with a rifle. We had lessons on seamanship, and classes in the rate you would be striking. I was assigned to be a fireman striker, and Frank was assigned a seaman striker. If you don't already know, a striker in the Navy is like a person working as an apprentice.

The qualifications for a fireman striker consisted of knowing Navy seamanship, the fireman rate, and included classes on all type of Navy knots, flags, oil fired engines, and anything else that had to be known about running the power plant of ships.

This all started because of my older brother Lou's brilliant idea for me to join before I turned eighteen. He talked Frank (who was eighteen) and me into joining the Reserves. "It'd be great extra money..." he said. His famous saying, "if there's to be a war, we'd probably be doing mine sweeping duty on the East Coast."

At the time we signed up for the Reserves, Lou, who was also attached to our unit, had already been called up for active duty.

1

Anyway, that's Lou for you.

At our first drill session, we were issued a full sea bag of US Navy clothing consisting of blues, whites, dungarees, hats, underwear, hammock with blankets, and other miscellaneous items. Everything had to be stenciled with our name or initials, and they also had to be rolled according to the Navy Blue Jacket Manual.

While most of my friends were playing at Easton's Beach, my brother and I continued with our training. In the summer of 1940, most of our unit who hadn't been called to active duty went on a two week cruise aboard the USS Williams (DD108). This ship was an old four stacker, which didn't have very many modern conveniences and was mainly used to train us reserves.

We went aboard the USS Williams on July 24, 1940. I was assigned to the fire gang, and Frank was topside with the seamen.

When I told my parents I wanted to be a fireman, this isn't what I was talking about.

I was stationed in the fireroom with two other men, and our work schedule when we were underway was four hours on and eight hours off.

While underway, we manned the oil burners and made sure we were creating enough steam pressure. When the engine room requested more pressure for more speed, or whatever, we had to ensure the pressure was there for them.

If we had the wrong mix of oil and air it would create a lot of black smoke, and they would alert us by banging on the deck.

Upon my very first shift, I knew immediately why we worked in the fireroom for only four hours. The heat down there was extreme, sweat dripped down our faces, pouring out of every pore on our bodies. It soaked our clothing until we could practically wring a bucket of water out of the uniforms.

Taking salt pills was a necessity, unless we wanted to end up out cold and face first on the floor of the ship. As for ventilation, the air coming from topside was very limited. When we were through with our shift, we'd take a quick shower, fresh water was at a premium, and our time was limited.

During those two weeks, we sailed from Newport Harbor to Norfolk, VA for mine sweeping exercises. I could hear Lou's voice in my head, "See, I told you that you'd be doing mine sweeping duty on the East Coast."

At Norfolk we boarded an old Eagle Boat built by Ford that they used in WWI. It was set up with a fish, a buoy-type canister shaped like a fish. The fish would be dragged through the water by a cable attached to the ship. It had cutters on it so when it would catch a mine cable, it'd be able to cut through and the mine would surface. We continuously launched the fish until everyone was proficient in its capabilities. (Some cutters had small explosive charges.)

Lunch on board, cold cuts slapped between two pieces of bread, what the Navy calls an H C sandwich. It didn't turn out too well for a few of the men. They'd gotten sick, possibly from the sandwiches. We secured for the day, leaving Hampton Roads and returned to the USS Williams.

From Norfolk, we traveled at night, and we ran into a storm on Chesapeake Bay. I was on duty in the fireroom at the time. The ship was actually leaving the water and we could feel it shake, grinding, and screaming on its return to the water. We held on to anything that'd keep us from falling; the storm had taken control of the ship.

When I got off duty, I looked around for my

brother, Frank. Going topside, you could see the damage the storm had caused to the ship. He said it'd been pretty bad.

During the two weeks aboard the USS Williams, we were given liberty in Washington, DC. I saw the Capital and a few other tourist attractions.

My pay for the two weeks was $9.80. At seventeen, I'd thought I was making darn good money. It wasn't too bad at all. The pay for recruits, at that time, was $21.00 a month.

Our tour was completed August 9, 1940.

NAVAL RESERVE UNIT
GETS ORDERS FOR DUTY

Ninth Division to Report for Active Service May 19

General Terry on Tactical Inspection Tour of Harbor Forts; Navy Gets Quonset Land

The Ninth Division, Naval Reserves, composed of Newporters, has received orders to report for active duty May 19 at the Naval Training Station here, Lieutenant Commander Walter E. Quinlan, commanding officer, announced. After an intensive period of training and instruction the division will be transferered to a local defense activity in the First Naval District.

This is the second Newport company to go on active duty in recent weeks, Company F, 118th Engineers, Rhode Island National Guard, now being at Camp Blanding, Fla., in training with the 43rd Division.

Orders to the Newport Naval Reserve unit culminate a waiting period that began last October, when the unit was placed on "stand by" orders for active duty. Since that time all men have received complete outfits of naval clothing, includng hammocks, and instructions given in marking and stowing clothes preparatory to reporting for active duty.

Under present plans, the division will march from the State Armory to the Government Landing at 8 A. M., Monday, May 19, to be taken to the Training Station. A preliminary physical examination has been given all men, and it is not believed many will be rejected when the final rigid physical examination is given.

General Terry Inspects

Major General Thomas A. Terry, commanding the First Coast Artillery District, arrived at Fort Adams today with members of his staff for a tactical in-

1941

On May 12, 1941 our unit was called to active duty. I was in my senior year at Rogers. I was so close to graduation. There was nothing I could do to change the orders. I'd signed up in the Reserves and that's the way it goes.

Our unit reported to the US Naval Training Station in Newport, RI for boot training.

Chief Yarbrough was our leading chief for the seven weeks we were there. At boot camp our unit was integrated with the reserve unit from Pawtucket, RI. At the station we had to complete the full requirement of training.

We reported to Barracks D and were confined in the detention area for the first two weeks. After detention, we moved to Barracks A. Once we were in the barracks, we were free to go about the base. The Navy kept us pretty busy, but we were still able to have liberty on the weekends. I made a quick stop home and took off to shoot the bull with our friends before heading back.

For our training with firearms, our unit went to the Navy shooting range at Third Beach where we learned how to handle the 303 rifle and the BAR rifle. The BAR is an automatic rifle that's not quite a traditional rifle but not quite a machine gun either. With the Browning automatic rifle, it's possible to either shoot off a single shot or select the full automatic firing mode. We had to do both. It was quite an experience. We also went out to the skeet range and shot birds (disks).

Every Friday we had full inspection of our gear and barracks. On Saturdays, all units march in front of the Naval War College. As all the units march off the field, the band would play The Beer Barrel Polka.

One day after a march, we returned to our barracks and Chief Yarbrough told us that we were supposed to sing along with the band. On the following Saturday, we sang loud and clear.

He was happy.

We also won the right to fly the best unit flag. The best unit flag is awarded weekly, and it was kind of a big deal.

The USS Constellation was docked at the pier for two nights. Our unit stayed aboard for both nights. Sleeping accommodations were in our hammock below deck. Matter of fact, it was the first time I used a hammock. We're required to carry it with us whenever we travel.

Some of the people from RI attached to our unit: my brother Frank, Vic Marcucci, Bob Hagensen (Red), Jim Burke, John McGann, and George Young.

Of course, there were others, but these are the guys I had contact with as my time in the service continues.

Frank and Vic were sent to NAS Jacksonville, FL to attend Aviation Metalsmith School. Joe, Jim, John, George, and a few from the Pawtucket unit (can't recall their names), and I was sent to Aviation Radio School at NAS Sand Point in Seattle, WA.

It was a long and interesting trip to get to Sand Point NAS. No commercial flights for us, we had to take a train.

On June 24th, we left Newport in an open stake body truck. There were a lot of people there to see us off and say our good-byes. My sister Mary and my mother were among the well-wishers.

The truck took us to Melville where we boarded a train that took us to Providence, then on to New York. In New York, we boarded a Pullman train that brought us to Seattle. It took three days to go cross-country with stops at Chicago and Denver.

When we arrived in Seattle, we were transported to NAS Sand Point. We arrived just in time to start classes the first of July. The Aviation Radio School was new and we were the second class to attend.

Aviation Radio classes consisted of learning how to type at least 40 wpm, take and receive Morse code at 30 wpm or higher, semaphore (flags), blinker (flashing light) and we had to learn how to fire up radio gear that was being used in naval aviation.

I think typing without looking at the keys was the biggest challenge for me. Morse code, along with specific code words, was like learning another language.

We had Saturday leave and went to check out some joints and shoot the bull with our new mates. Then back to the grindstone, memorizing all the blinkers, signals, and flags. I needed to practice my speed with tapping in the Morse codes, too.

It was a grind, but I succeeded and graduated on October 24th. Our weekends were normally our own, and I took the time to study up until this point. After I was more confident in my codes and signals I started to relax a little.

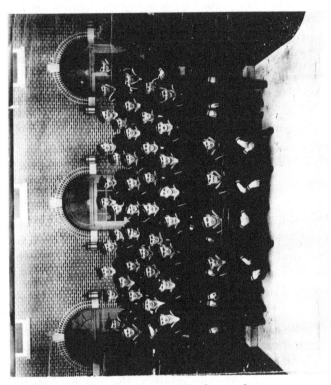

Aviation School
Graduation Class
H. P. Lawrence
(top row, last man on the right)

A group of us took a bus to Seattle for liberty. Seattle was a very clean city and the people were very hospitable. In Seattle, I saw my first college football game and I saw Count Basie at one of the theaters.

Of course, I didn't go on liberty every weekend, only when I had money.

On November 3rd, we left Seattle by train for my next duty station...Hawaii. We arrived on the 4th at Mare Island, a naval base in San Pablo Bay north of San Francisco, and stayed overnight.

We were transported by a stake body truck to San Francisco to meet with the USS Downes (DD375), USS Cassin (DD372), and USS Shaw (DD373) which were waiting to take us to the Hawaiian Islands.

On November 12th, we sailed for Hawaii and arrived on the 19th. While on board the USS Downes, I was assigned as a messenger on the bridge.

After our arrival at Pearl Harbor, we were taken by whale boat to Ford Island. My orders were that I was assigned to VP 22, Bob Hagensen was also assigned to VP 22.

They dropped us off at the barracks which was facing the harbor. It was a beautiful view with most of the battleships tied up at buoys alongside of the island. The barracks were quite empty at the time because the squadron was away at Midway.

Our sleeping quarters were on the second floor and the mess hall was on the first. We had to check in to our squadron each morning.

Red and I were assigned to the radio shack and were kept busy doing multiple assignments.

My first holiday in the Navy was Thanksgiving. We had the day off. The Thanksgiving meal was a dinner to remember.

It just seems odd. Before I joined the Naval

Reserves, the farthest I was away from my parents or home was a couple of summer vacations in Taunton on my cousin's farm. I'd made a couple of day trips to Uxbridge, and also went to visit my brother, Manny, who was living on Long Island.

Now, I found myself six thousand miles away from home.

While on liberty, we hit a couple of joints, got to know some of the locals, and enjoyed their company.

I wasn't very lonesome. I think the regimentation in the service helped a lot, letters from home, and just having fun, keeping busy.

Red and I were together a lot which also helped.

As I go along with this writing, I find that the service is a very funny place. In a way, I got to know a lot of people, but didn't really know them that well.

The place filled up pretty quick when the squadron that was at Midway returned December 5th.

December 7th started like any other Sunday in the service for me. Since it was my day off, I slept in, which means I didn't have breakfast. I was planning on going to a later mass at the Chapel and just wanted to enjoy a lazy day, eat a quick lunch afterwards, and shoot the bull with the guys.

I remember being slightly aggravated because there was so much noise and I was being rudely awakened from a wonderfully sound sleep.

Everything seemed muffled at first and then the next thing that I heard was a loud noise. I practically fell out of bed, and jumped up to see what was going on. As I ran toward the window, someone said that we were being attacked by the Japs.

You have to understand, all of this took seconds, split seconds that seemed to be in slow motion— watching a train wreck that couldn't be stopped. Every second was engraved in my eyes and brain as each movement was pulling me forward.

I ran to the balcony in my shorts where I had an excellent view of the harbor. The unmistakable sound of multiple airplane bombers coming at us thundered in my ears.

Looking up, I could see large formations of aircraft going to other targets. As I turned my head to look over the harbor, the Jap torpedo planes and dive bombers had a nice clean run at the Battleships.

With each drop of their torpedoes and bombs, I could feel the percussion of the explosions as they annihilated everything on Battleship row.

Some of the men on the ships were firing back, but it was a losing battle. Without any opposition, the Japs had everything going their way.

It was damned sad.

The clear air over the harbor was encompassed

with smoke, and the clean water was turning black with oil.

Those of us in the barracks knew we had to get down to the squadron and report in. I don't remember when I grabbed my clothes, or how I managed to dress while I was watching the destruction unfold before my eyes.

As I slipped in my shoes, a bright flash blinded me. Looking over toward Battleship Row, flames were licking the oil in the harbor.

Just about that time there was another large explosion and I could see the Arizona was on fire. The black smoke from her went straight up into the sky. The Battleships tied up at Ford Island were starting to settle to the bottom.

Our squadron was about a half mile from the barracks. On our way down the road leading to our squadron, we'd ducked for cover a few times. After the Japs dropped their bombs they started strafing.

Someone would yell and we'd hit the dirt. You could see them coming with their guns firing, but we all reported in without anyone getting hit.

The dry docks across the harbor from our barracks were in flames. I hadn't known it then, but the USS Downes was one of the ships that was hit. (The Downes was in dry dock at the time Pearl was bombed.)

Our squadron and all the planes that we had parked two days ago were destroyed. The hanger we shared with VP21 had a couple of large gaping holes.

Since we were still under attack, the strafing aircraft kept us moving as quickly as possible. We had to get the burning planes away from the ones that weren't on fire.

All of a sudden it was dead silent. There was an

eerie stillness, a numbness after hearing all the explosions. All I could see around the harbor was burning ships. There were a lot of small whale boats and fishing boats picking up men from the oil blackened water.

The smell was something I don't think I'll ever forget. The stench of burning oil and destruction...

Someone from our squadron suggested for me to set up a fifty caliber machine gun in one of the PBY's. He asked if I'd ever shot one and I said no.

I learned real quick how to shoot one.

We moved the PBY over to the opening of the hanger, positioning it so we could shoot and protect the airplane as much as possible.

We ended up relieving each other, taking turns being on look-out, etc. I was on the ground after we loaded the machine gun.

Just about then the Japs returned. This time they were doing a lot more strafing. When the Jap planes started coming in our direction, we started firing the fifty that we'd just loaded.

How a handful of seconds could feel like eternity, I don't know. But it sure felt like an eternity to me. All I could do was stand near the opening of the hanger, watch, and point to any aircraft coming our way.

I'll tell you right now, when they came back the second time around, anyone that had a gun was firing it.

During all this mess, the USS Nevada, which had gotten up steam was coming up the channel, and ran itself into a sandbar in the middle of the harbor on purpose. I think they did it so the ship wouldn't sink in the harbor, and foul up the channel.

When the strafing ended, they mentioned the men from the ships would be needing clothing. I left the squadron area and went up to the barracks to open my locker.

For some reason or other I went through the mess hall.

That was a huge mistake. I just couldn't seem to get this out of my head.

Every table in the mess hall had a body on it. They were all covered with oil and blood. The medics were working as fast as they could to help and relieve their pain. Seeing this, watching the medics, kicked in the reality of what was happening around me.

I swear I started sweating it out right there.

I ran to my locker and brought down everything I could spare. Handing them to the guy who was collecting the items for the sailors, I turned to the squadron leader for more direction.

He had everyone moving planes around and cleaning up the hanger. We broke out the thirty and fifty caliber ammo, and started linking them in belts so we'd be ready for when they came back. Most of us couldn't believe how old the ammo was (WW1), and we all hoped they'd work.

Our ships were gone.

All the ships that'd been tied up at Ford Island were on the bottom of the harbor or close to it. Men were putting out the fires, and starting the pumps to get the water out. After taking inventory of what happened on Ford Island, it told us the Japs had knocked out all our Battleships, and two of them went belly up.

Over in the dry dock area, billowing smoke was visible from the ships that were hit. The USS Arizona was still smoking, its forward mast was starting to bend because of the intense heat.

It was a complete loss.

The fishing and whale boats from the island residents were still cruising the harbor, trying to save whoever was left, picking up bodies, and taking pictures.

All three PBY squadrons VP22, 23, and 24 lost most of their planes. My squadron, the VP22 didn't have any planes that were able to fly. All three squadrons were crippled.

The Japs had hit outside of the hanger we shared with VP 21, and also disabled all of our planes on the ramp.

We had nothing left and would have to wait for replacements from the States, for planes and ships to be built before we could defend ourselves.

Time was a factor we couldn't control.

The day went by pretty fast, they kept us busy doing a little of this and that. When evening rolled around we ate some dry sandwiches. So much had happened that it wasn't until then I realized I hadn't eaten all day. Dry as they were, those sandwiches tasted good.

They mentioned there was a water truck on the strip so Red (Bob Hagensen) and I went looking. As we were out on the strip, with a blink of an eye, the sky lit up with gunfire.

There was a spattering of gunfire everywhere, all day, and I think I was finally scared. I don't think I had time to be scared earlier that morning. There was no time to think, just time to do.

Red and I couldn't find the water tank. We had to beat it back to the squadron area once the gunfire had started again.

We found out later a few of our own planes were trying to land at Ford.

It was pretty late by this time and the word came

down that we might as well turn in for the night.

The day after the Japs bombed us, actually the next morning, I didn't know where we were going to eat. They said the mess hall was open so we headed down there.

I couldn't believe my eyes. Everything was clean, it took a few seconds to get it out of my head, but we chowed down. It was like I never saw all those sailors and medics—like they'd never even been there.

However, after breakfast I looked out over the harbor, and saw the mess the attack had created.

Reality was back.

They already had work crews working on the ships. Water was being pumped out of the ships and men were working with torches, working at a maddening pace to get everything literally shipshape again.

A few days after the Japs bombed Pearl, they let us go into Honolulu so we could send telegrams home to let our families know we were all right.

USS Shaw

USS Arizona

Attack on Pearl Harbor
December 7, 1941

1942

To our pleasant surprise, within a couple of weeks after the attack, replacement planes started arriving. Boy, we sure were relieved to see them.

I was assigned to ground crew before they put me on a flight crew.

The PBY-5 Catalinas are flying boats. Once they arrived, we launched and recovered aircraft when they returned from their schedule flight.

On launch, we had to remove the two side wheels and the rear wheel, all while the aircraft's in the water with their engines idling. When we return, they put the wheels back on, and the recovery vehicle takes them from the boat ramp to their parking area or the hanger.

I was put on a flight crew as a second radioman for about a week, then assigned to pull mess duty. The squadron pulled out while I was on mess duty for the South Pacific (Dutch East Indies).

After mess duty I was put on a flight crew again, as second radioman, and started drawing flight skins. That meant I received a 50% increase in pay.

About this time, we were all issued gas masks we had to carry with us at all times. The whole unit was in a blue bag with a shoulder strap. It was very bulky, and they were a pain in the neck.

Can't remember if I mentioned this before, but I was assigned to VP22 in November of 1941, and was transferred to VP 24.

They had scheduled me for Pat Wing Two Radio School.

I entered Pat Wing Two Radio School in March, and graduated in May 1942. It was a constant deluge of new words, distinctions, and codes. The hard part was that there was a lot of stuff we couldn't take out of the classroom, we had to learn it all right there.

I imagined it'd be an ongoing thing, since the Japs had a way of breaking our codes. We'd be learning new stuff all the time.

This school was about the same as the one in Seattle, but they're pushing some pretty heavy training on the equipment we'd be using in the PBYs.

After radio school, I was sent to Pat Wing One Gunnery School at Kaneohe Bay from May to June. It was quite an extensive course.

Day 1—bomb and torpedo racks.

Day 2—sighting and recognitions of enemy aircraft and ships.

Day 3 & 4—strip and learn all about 30cal and 50cal machine guns, and they also threw in small arms. I was qualified to wear a machine gunners patch!

The squadron had advanced duty bases at Midway and also Johnston Island. Unfortunately, I have no flight log book, no recording of time flown. Most of our flights were patrols.

We had a hurricane flight, in which we flew right through the eye and out the other side. It was a pretty rough ride.

I remember staring at the walls of the plane wondering if the hurricane force winds would rip us, and the walls apart. The plane shook like we were a box being kicked down the street. I kept picturing (like the cartoons and funny papers), the rivets working their way out and pinging me in the head.

I completely understand what people mean when they say a white-knuckled moment.

While at school, half of VP24 was sent to Midway. The rest of us, including me, were put on stand-by They're calling it the Battle of Midway which happened in the early part of June, the 3-6th.

After school in June, I was put on another flight crew. PBY radio equipment consisted of two radio receivers (RU1) which had removable coils that gave you access to the frequency you needed.

A frequency meter lined up the correct frequency. The radio transmitter (GO9), and a directional radio antenna had to be turned by hand.

The antennas were on the wing between the two engines. The radio and transmitter antennas were strung from one wing to the tail and other wing with a lead in between the wing to tail to our radio station.

There was also a trailing wire antenna that we had to set up. Here you'd have to take out a shut off assembly that went to the bottom of the aircraft, and put in the trailing wire assemble into the pipe tube.

We also had a voice receiver/transmitter that the pilot used when he was in range for landing and takeoff. (Distance was line of sight or a little better)

My duties as a radioman were pretty straight forward. A radioman assured all of the radio equipment's was operable. After takeoff, we'd report that we were airborne. When on patrol we'd send CW signal in Morse code to let them know we were airborne.

We're required to stand watch on that frequency,

and also set up the other receiver to listen for emergency signals. Also, we had to listen in on the intercom if we were needed.

Intercom and emergency frequency in one ear, and frequency watch in the other. It took a little while to get used to, but if anything came in from the base you would normally cut off the other two. This way you could keep your full attention on receiving Morse code.

I saw my brother, Lou, the first time since I left home June 15, 1942. We went on liberty and he also gave me a tour of his ship, the USS San Diego. The San Diego was just commissioned, and she had all modern equipment on it.

It really was great.

Since I've been with the VP24, I've flown about 300 hours as 2nd Radioman, so far. We had a two week tour at Midway in early July, from July 5th through July 17th.

When we got there, they still hadn't done any repairs to the island. The Japs had completely demolished everything on the ground. They'd just put up tents for our living quarters, and a far as the mess hall was concerned, they cooked everything out in the open in large pots.

They issued us our own eating gear metal folded plate, a metal cup with water canteen, and silverware. After we finished eating we had to wash our gear in large heated fifty gallon drums of hot water.

No water for showers so most of us used the ocean for our bathing with salt water soap.

The latrines were plain holes in the ground with a couple of boards so you could sit down. Like camping out, definitely a bit on the primitive side.

As far as recreation was concerned, we played with

the Gooney Birds (Albatross). We'd capture one and swing it to see if we could get it to fly. Most of the time they'd fall flat on their face. Such fun with the birds.

Watching the Gooney Birds was a riot. We laughed so hard watching some of them land, the muscles on my sides hurt the next day. They're huge. So graceful flying in the air, but when they go to land—all that gracefulness? Poof! Gone! I about busted a gut laughing.

They'd put their feet out to land and tumble onto the ground in every which way, head over tails, flapping, and gawking loudly. I was surprised they didn't break their necks or wings. Some of them would just stop and lay there after they tumbled all over the place.

Unfortunately, they were a hazard for our planes. Especially on landing and take-off; a couple of our planes had been hit, and they'd make a large dent on the aircraft leading edge. Which, of course, happened to us. It put the aircraft out of service until it was fixed.

Most of our patrols were ten hour hops. On one patrol, we took a couple of marines with us and they enjoyed the ride very much. They'd sit in the blister (where the gunner sits) and stand our watches.

I got friendly with this one sergeant, and saw him one time later in one of the bars in town.

I was sitting having a drink and this marine who just came from the states started giving me a hard time. The sergeant saw what was going on and told the kid to take off. I wish I could remember his name, but he was with the first division.

I heard later that in August he was shipped to the Canal (Guadalcanal) in the Solomon Islands with the first Marine division. They've been doing a series of air, ground, and sea actions. I hoped he was safe.

Since we didn't stay on any particular island for very long, when we were returned to Ford Island they gave us R&R at the Royal Hawaiian Hotel. Boy, this was really great! (The price on the door for that room was $110. Can you imagine?)

We had our own room shared with a buddy. The eating facilities were memorable. The dining room had a beautiful view of Waikiki beach, and if you wanted to go swimming all you had to do was go out the back door and you'd be in the ocean. The beach was very flat and it was a long walk in the water to get over my head.

On September 4th to the 14th, we had a two week tour at Johnson Island. Just about the time the Air Force made a PR bombing run to Wake Island.

We were sent out from Johnson Island to a point that would give the Air Force a CW signal so they would know where they were if they lost their bearing. (CW-continuous wave)

After this tour, we had R&R again at the Royal Hawaiian. We had a bunch of fun, shooting the bull, playing around. It was definitely needed. Once that was done, everyone was ready to get back to work.

Most of our flights out of Ford Island were patrols and practice landings. On one of the patrols, we had a fire in the electrical junction box in the radio compartment.

I opened the box and the fire was starting to reach for the overhead.

We started emptying CO_2 bottles to keep the fire down. I put all the switches on the junction box to the 'off' position, hoping it'd help. After that, I disconnected the DC Battery which was under the radio seat hoping again with everything off that the fire would expend itself.

The fire finally burned itself out. One of the relays in the box had shorted causing the fire. We headed back to base without any more problems, but I was scared, because if the fire had gotten out of control, it would've gone up to the wings where our gas tanks were. If that had happened we would've been goodbye.

Flying with VP24, all our aircraft were PBY 5s. The only thing new that was added to the aircraft was RADAR and an IFF box. The RADAR didn't work well as the antenna was a bunch of sticks attached to the bow of the aircraft with antenna wire strung across these sticks.

They also installed a friend or foe box (IFF) which sent out a signal to let them know we weren't the enemy.

Last but not least, we're seaplanes, and had to land in the channel of Pearl Harbor. When we approached our landing ramp a crew would be sent out to attach portable wheels; one on each side of the aircraft and one in the rear.

Once the wheels were attached, a tow truck would pull us up the ramp, and then park the aircraft. It's probably the reason they had transferred all squadrons (seaplane) on Ford Island to Kaneohe Bay. The harbor was getting very busy with ships coming in and out.

I was with VP 24 from February to September 1942. I have no idea how many flights we went on. I didn't record any of it.

The squadron received the Presidential Unit Citation. Also, I made 3rd class petty officer while assigned to this squadron.

In September, when VP24 was transferred to Kaneohe, I was transferred to HEDRON FAW 2, and was expected to be there until June 1943.

While with HEDRON, I was checking out as 1st Radioman in the PBYs, PB2Ys, PBMs, and PB4Ys (B24s). The PB4Ys aren't seaplanes. I also had to work on small types of aircraft.

And just so you understand, I didn't fly the planes, I was a radioman—just a radioman. Although, I'd been crossed trained in RADAR, gunnery, and could work in the blister when needed.

I had to go back and learn more codes. Japs keep breaking our codes. I felt a bit out of place. I swear I was the only one in the group that was not an Indian. (American-Indian)

It'd been extremely busy those last few months, a lot of flights, night and day.

We've had a few headaches with the PBYs. They're always having generator trouble. Usually the planes took off early in the morning, before the sunrise. They'd call us, and we'd have to go fix the generator.

There were two things that we could do depending on the type of problem. We could take the generator out or fix the clutch which would slip. This meant we'd have to set up the portable staging, and take the small cowling off the engine so we could get to the generator.

They'd start the engine again, and we sat on the staging, and adjust the clutch. It got easier after a while—after you got over the fear of falling off this small staging which was actually attached to the engine.

Other times if the engine wouldn't start we'd have to get up on the engine with a large crank and crank it until the engine started. The tricky part here was not to fall off the wing.

The propeller was turning, and you had to pull out the crank. (The crank was about three feet long) The worse part, even with the engine idling, was getting to the walkway which was between the two engines, and getting back down to the ground or the blister.

So far, I've put in about 90 hours in flying time since I've been with HEDRON FAW 2; some testing aircraft or flying so pilots could get their flight time in.

There'd been some pretty hot fighting over on the Pacific side, a few close calls, but we were doing what we needed to do.

Christmas 1942, my sister Mary sent me a small, Virgin Mary medallion which I still wear.

Hawaii
U. S. A.

Christmas Day

1942

* * * *

U. S. NAVAL AIR STATION
Kaneohe Bay, Oahu, T. H.

W. M. DILLON,
Captain, U. S. Navy,
Commanding

R. C. WARRACK,
Commander, U. S. Navy,
Executive Officer

H. R. COOKE,
Lieutenant (sc), USNR,
Commissary Officer

ANTHONY LORENZ,
Pay Clerk, U. S. Navy,
Asst. Comm. Officer

H. C. PUDCHUN,
CCStd., U.S.N.

* * * *

Menu

✻ ✻ ✻ ✻

Fruit Cup

Ripe Olives   Celery Hearts, Stuffed

Pickles

ROAST TOM TURKEY

BAKED SPICED HAM

Southern Corn Bread Dressing

Giblet Gravy   Cranberry Sauce

Mashed Potatoes   Peas

Asparagus Salad   Thousand Island Dressing

Hot Mince Pie   Ice Cream

Parker House Rolls   Butter

Coffee

Candy and Mixed Nuts

Cigars and Cigarettes

✻ ✻ ✻ ✻

I got a touch of malaria. Not sure which island I contracted it on. Who knows? We hop from island to island and never stay on one for very long. We had to keep moving around so we won't be found.

They were looking hard for us Cats.

I was promoted to 2nd Radioman. Most of my flights had been on the PBYs but I was still assigned to the flight crews on the other planes I mentioned before.

WITH FOUR SONS EACH IN SERVICE

These Newport mothers are, left to right, Mrs. Jennie E. Brawner of 1 West Howard street, Mrs. Mary S. Lawrence of 18 Dearborn street, and Mrs. Luiza Furtado of 20 Willow street. The women attended the recent dedication exercises at the Roll of Honor at the city hall. —Kerschner Photo.

Lou, Frank, and myself, were in the Navy. Hap (Joe) joined the Merchant Marine.

Red had a tour of duty in the South Pacific and was back in the states.

I also saw George Young, who just completed a tour of the South Pacific. We had quite a bull session the night before he flew back to the States. His squadron left Kaneohe the next day, and unfortunately, the plane that George was on never made it back.

It takes approximately twenty hours of flying time to get back to the States. (California)

With that loss, the Navy had stopped all squadrons from taking the PBY aircraft back. It'd been a long trip home even after the flight. After landing in California, we had to travel across the country to get back to Newport.

Victory at the Canal!

The battles at the Canal were pretty much over. The Japs had evacuated the island. I may have mentioned this before, I preferred the older PBY-5s, the weight of the gear in the 5As were heavier, and had given us less power and range.

Some of VP-24 had been transferred to Espiritu Santo. At HEDRON FAW 2, I was doing Dumbo runs, night flights, bounces, and other assorted missions.

1943

I know I've said this before but, I think the Merchant Marines get the wrong end of the deal, and a lot less credit than they should be getting.

Almost everything we need arrives by ship, ships manned by the Merchant Marines. It was just as dangerous for them as it was for any of the other armed services.

These men put their lives on the line every day. Many of the seamen were "too old" to join the regular armed services, didn't have good hearing, or couldn't see that well–things that the armed services rejected. So, some of them joined the Merchant Marines.

As far as I know, their ships weren't armed. If they're approached by enemy ships or planes, they had no way to defend themselves.

They were sitting ducks!

It took a lot of courage to take to the seas during war time without being able to defend yourself against attacks. I'm sure there were some who were captured, became POWs that we didn't hear about.

I got myself assigned to VP71 as a 1st Radioman on a flight crew. I figured I was never going to get back to the states, and if I pulled a tour down south I would at least get leave.

I also had a choice to join a PBY4Y squadron, also known as B24s. I didn't particularly care for this aircraft when I worked on them, and since they gave me a choice, I went with VP71.

We've got an incredible team. Lt. Cmdr. C.K. Harper, USN was made commanding officer of VP71 Nine crews made up the nucleus. Lt. Cmdr. Sears took the remaining crews to form VB104 a Navy liberator squadron that used the PBY4Ys.

We didn't train long at Kaneohe, as most of our training was gunnery and bombing torpedo runs, including night water bounce, high altitude bombing at Lanai, and also checking out RADAR.

We were now flying the PBY5c which were a new series of seaplanes, equipped with a better RADAR antenna system, and one new radio receiver which was then called a super heterodyne (ARR 1). We didn't have to change coils with the new radio receiver; my second receiver was still the old type (RU1). Otherwise nothing else was new. We trained from June 12th to the 20th.

We left Kaneohe on June 21st for Palmyra Atoll (Satapuala Base). We had to make a stop at Upolu Samoa (Western Samoa). The pitch control was giving us a problem, and we had to lay over for a replacement part. The pitch control was pretty important, and we couldn't fly without it working properly.

The easiest way to explain is, there are three different types of motion that affects the airplane's center of gravity. Roll, pitch, and yaw.

One takes care of the front to back axis (roll), one takes care of the vertical axis (yaw), and then, the pitch takes care of the side-to-side axis.

All three must be working properly in order for the plane to have the proper center of gravity.

Liberty was spent in Apia, Samoa; the island where Robert Louis Stevenson lived. The natives on the island were still living in huts and were very friendly. I met a native who knew Stevenson, and we had quite a bull session.

After we fixed our aircraft we caught up to the rest of the squadron in Espiritu Santo, New Hebrides Island. There we boarded the USS Curtiss (AV-4) which was a seaplane tender, June 29. It was our home base for a while.

On July 2nd, our first patrol, we were supposed to go to Vanikoro, which was an advanced base approximately 230 miles north of Espiritu. We never arrived there as our compasses weren't working properly. It was quite a while before we realized that something was wrong.

Ens. Cocks asked me if I could do anything. The first thing I tried was our DF (Direction Finder), which was also out as it wouldn't give me a true north or south null indication.

I tried RADAR next. This didn't work either as we were too far out for long range search.

Just about this time someone spotted a DD (Destroyer) on patrol, and we hailed it. No one else in the crew could take blinker so I was stuck with trying to receive any messages that I would request from them. I have to say, the Signalman aboard this ship was very patient with me after he realized my ability in receiving blinker was very poor.

Trying to receive blinker at 1000 feet in the air from a ship that was bouncing around was quite a challenge!

We did get the information we were looking for, and as soon as we were headed in the right direction, I fired the DF up, sent the signal to Ens. Cocks, which was all we needed.

Usually patrols average around 10 hours, but this one lasted 14.4 hours. We were sweating the gas, wondering if we were going to ditch or not. As luck would have it, we landed safely back at Espiritu.

On the 4th of July, we transferred living quarters from the USS Curtiss to the USS Chandeleur (AV 10) which was also a seaplane tender. Most of our patrols were pretty normal, but as far as living aboard tenders, it was crowded. The ship personnel didn't care for it much either. It was quite a disruption for them because they had to cater to us.

Anytime we had to go to our aircraft—which was tied up at buoys in the harbor—they'd have to break out the boat and take us to our plane. They also had to deliver gas to our aircraft and load any armament that we'd need for our hop the next day.

I guess I should give you a little information about our dress code while flying. The enlisted men all wear dungarees, chambray shirts, work boots, which we called boon-dockers, sailor hats, and Mae West's (inflatable life jackets). The officers wear their khaki clothes.

We no longer wore leather helmets and goggles with the advent of the glass blister on the PBY5 series and up. Also, we didn't wear parachute harnesses as we never flew that high. Our normal flight height was about 1000 feet.

One other thing that I'd like to bring up is tying to a buoy. I liked doing this and had gotten pretty good at it.

First of all, I had to go to the front thirty caliber gun turret, open the top cover, climb out, and stand on the rail that was on the bow near the waterline.

Next, I opened the anchor compartment and pulled out the hook. The pilot would locate the buoy that we needed to tie up to. As we were going through the water, the men in the blister would be putting sea anchors out (collapsible canvas buckets with no bottom) which created a drag.

My job was to hook a small eye on the concrete anchor. Once I had accomplished this, I signaled the pilot to cut the engines.

Yes, the engines were running the whole time.

I then proceeded, to pull the hook out and put the permanent tie line in the eye of the anchor.

It was a bit of a challenge but I'd gotten pretty good at it.

Insigna Designed by
Milton Caniff

Black Cats were a PBY squadron that makes night flights. The PBYs are Catalinas…Cats. And they're painted a flat black so that we could fly at night and not be seen by the enemy.

I imagine it was pretty eerie for the Japs when we're near them. If it was cloudy, we'd use the clouds for cover and they couldn't see us. If it wasn't, we'd have to fly lower, closer to the water. When we flew close to the water, it was dangerous, but, they weren't looking down for us, they were looking up, so we had the element of surprise.

Someone told me a while back, the Japs thought we were a mysterious secret weapon because they couldn't see us.

We've been busy here in the South Pacific. The day after my birthday, on October 11th, on a preflight check, we found a gas leak. The only place that it could be fixed was at Ile Nou, New Caledonia.

While waiting for our plane to be fixed we had liberty in Noumea, New Caladonia. Living conditions were primitive. We stayed in tents.

A few days later, we moved to Halavo Bay RNZAF Base on Florida Island, in the Solomon Islands. (New Zealand Air Force) There were about fifteen PBYs operating from this base. This base was just across from Guadalcanal.

The living quarters weren't too bad as we were set up in the new Quonset Huts, and living conditions were pretty good.

VPB 71 Black Cat Squadron
Black Eagle Crew

For some reason they called this base Todd City. I haven't found out why.

From this point on things got away from being routine.

We made a Dumbo run to Rendova, (West of Guadalcanal), and picked up a marine Captain with two Japs he'd captured, and brought them back to base for interrogation.

It was the first time I saw the enemy up close. The Captain kept them in the bunk area. They had the most beautiful black eyes that I ever saw.

The next day, we carried six New Zealander RADAR men to set up gear at Empress Augusta Bay. From there, we transported a Major and Captain of the marines, and dropped them off at Treasury Island.

At Treasury Island, we transported a marine Captain and Sergeant (SBD crew) who had lost their plane and dropped them off at Rendova.

November 24th, we moved from Todd City to the USS Coos Bay tender (AVP 25). The Coos Bay was a small tender and living conditions were crowded again. She was anchored in Halavo Bay, which was called Halavo Seaplane Base.

We did do a lot of hopping back and forth.

We took three officers and three enlisted men to Rendova where they plotted to lay buoys.

Then back for another Dumbo run to Empress Augusta Bay. We picked up three stretcher cases plus a Commander, Major, and three Lieutenants.

With the eight of them in the seaplane, we made a quick transport to Vella Lavella which is northwest of Guadalcanal. We dropped off the injured there and then brought the officers back to Rendova.

While transporting them from the water launch to the plane I accidentally put my fingers in the bullet holes in one of the injured man's back.

He let me know about it. I felt bad, horrible. I wasn't thinking about anything except moving—we had to move, and we had to move fast.

While all this was going on the Japs were shelling us from shore. On most of these Dumbo hops, we usually had air coverage so when we landed on the water we wouldn't be sitting ducks.

There were a few nighttime patrols toward Bougainville. We also did some spotting for DDs, so they could lob shells onto the Island where the Japs were holed up.

At Halavo Bay we were still doing a lot of Dumbo runs, along with day and night patrols. We made a couple of runs to the Canal to drop passengers off, searched a sector that a B24 was supposed to have been ditched.

We also checked on a ship that was in distress, but she said they could make it back to the base.

During this time, there were a couple of close calls with unidentified planes. We were very glad to make it back.

We also ran into a couple of storms. I thought one of them was going to rip the wings off the plane.

That's how bad it was!

It felt like the time when I was with VP24 and we were tracking a hurricane and flew directly into the eye. Between the hurricanes and the instruments going wacky, sometimes it makes me wonder how we managed to limp back to home base.

1944

On February 19th, we moved from the Coos Bay to the USS Wright (AV 1). We've continued doing Patrols from Halavo.

As you can imagine, this moving around was a pain. Anytime we wanted anything from our plane, we had to get a boat and be transported. It was always hot and the planes when you got to them they were steaming. You have to realize also that we're pretty close to the Equator, too.

Also quinine's the pill of the day. Any problems, they give us quinine.

I finally got my orders to go on leave!

About twenty of us were transported to the Canal on March 6th.

We took a DC-3 to Espirito overnight. A couple of days later, we took a PBM-3 Pan-American to Funafuti—from Funafuti to Canton, Canton to Palmyra, Palmyra to Pearl. On our way to Pearl, we had an oil leak so we had to go back to Palmyra to have it fixed.

Started again this time and we made it to Pearl. Picked up a transport ship and landed in San Diego, California.

I haven't talked much about the guys so here's a list of the members of Crew 12

PPC Lt. (jg) Cocks Calif., Lt. (jg) A.J. Lehmicke Minn., Lt. (jg) Nickolas Calif.

PC W. Kern ACMM Ill., E. Eaddy AMM1/c N.C., H. Lawrence ARM 1/c R.I., G. Saxton ARM 1/c Penn transferred new crew in July 1st radioman, M. Mikula ARM 2/c Ohio, transferred new crew in Oct 1st radioman., A. Miller ARM2/c Al. transferred new crew in February, J. Becker ARM 2/c Col., R. Byk AMM 1/c Mass., C. White AOM 1/c., R. Barnett AMM 2/c came aboard in December as Mechanic. Kern's was transferred out and E.I. Eaddy was made PC in December.

I have to tell you, crossing the Equator and International Date Line was a big deal.

We were issued Flight Crew Wings for enlisted men—this was new. It was my first thirty-day leave since I left Newport on June 24, 1941.

Tour of overseas duty so far, twenty-eight months!

I couldn't believe I was lucky enough to see Frank while home on leave. He was stationed in Norfolk, VA. I'm glad he made it home. My brother, Hap, who's in the Merchant Marines, was also home.

My sister Mary and I went to Long Island to see my brother, Manny. He was working for Grumman Aircraft, and he gave me a tour of the plant he was working in, and other facilities of the company.

As Mary and I were on our way home to catch our train back to Providence, the taxi driver took us by the Empire State building. A couple of days before this a two engine bomber had run into the building and was still sticking out of one of the top floors.

At the end of June, after leave was over, my orders were to report back to HEDRON to North Island NAS, San Diego California.

In May 1944, I transferred from HEDRON San Diego to VPB 71. They were flying PBY-5As (Black

Cats). The 5As are amphibious aircraft. You may not know what Black Cats are, but they're painted all black, and most missions were flown at night.

The training programs began immediately for air and ground. Along with the routine flight training, we flew regular patrols. After training was completed we headed for NAS, Kaneohe Bay.

There were a few changes in our radio equipment. Instead of one RU receiver two new ARR receivers were installed. These new Super-Het receivers were much easier to use.

LORAN was also installed (long range navigation gear).

When we left the bay area, it was useless as there were no LORAN station for us to use. RADAR was much better. We had antennas on each side of the forward hull that we could control.

Also, we had the capability to install twin fifty canisters under each wing. They also installed twin thirties in our bow turret.

Our fifty calibers (in the blister) had a large reservoir for our ammo between our guns attached to the walkway. This was much better than the small one that was attached to the gun.

As far as clothing's concerned the only changes were a baseball cap, and a shoulder 38 caliber that was issued. Officers were now in flight suits. We were told that we'd get flight suits later.

Most of our hops were bounces off water and mat. There were some instrument and familiarization hops. We also had simulated ditch exercises, where they dropped you into the pool.

We'd be fully dressed with a parachute harness on sitting in a chair. They'd dump us into the water, and we'd have to take our harness off and return to the surface.

Of course, we were monitored. A couple of sailors would be under water when you were dumped.

They also made us pass a swimming course. Considering that I was born and raised on an island, all I could do was dog paddle, you'd think I'd have learned how to swim sooner.

We were issued 38s, and out to the range we went. At the range we had target shooting with the 38s and 45s, rapid and slow.

We'd continuously been doing more intense training missions, bounce RADAR, navigation, V flight, night formation, night bounce, gunnery, and finally after all that, we started flying with our own pilots and crew.

We were doing familiarization hops. Except for one night bounce, our front nose wheel collapsed on landing. Absolutely no one was hurt.

Our twin fifties, which were new, were installed under the wing had been working fine. Also, we'd had some practice doing torpedo runs and high altitude bombing.

We made a forced landing in Ensenada, Mexico on a small fighter strip for personal supplies for our trip south. We had to make a trip into town.

It took a while to get the aircraft squared away. It was quite a take-off as we had to run the engines at high speed, when we were ready to take off, both pilots released the brakes which gave us the speed needed...

We also started advice training flights, fighter evasive action, low attitude bombing, anti-submarine action with live depth charges, and using our new 50 caliber wing guns.

Preparing for flight to Hawaii, we had an extra rubberized tank installed in bunk department. This gave us more fuel to reach the islands. I may not have mentioned this before, we also had one of these tanks in our wing section.

For our trip to Hawaii, we had extra passengers and our gear plus records etc. The flight took us 19.3 hours to Hilo which was a short stop, and 1.5 hours to Kaneohe, our home base.

From mid-September to the day after my birthday, we were doing continuous training at Kaneohe Naval Air Station, then to advance duty at Midway until November. The detachment to Midway had six planes and nine crews which flew regular patrols and continued with gunnery training.

Most of the time we were flying patrols from Midway—except we lost one of our planes out there. They were later picked up, but we lost two men.

Nothing changed here except we had a mess hall to chow down in. Living arrangements were tents, but happily, we had a shower setup that we could use.

After Midway we continued training.

Mid-November, orders were received to report to Manus in the Admiralties, staging through Johnston and Kwajalein Islands.

We were finally on our way and didn't stop: We knew we couldn't stay in one place for long.

First hop to Johnston then to Kwajalein, trained in at Kwajalein for 3 days.

From Kwajalein to Manus then to Owi. We had four days rest there.

Owi to Biak and returned back to Owi.

Owi to Moratai, Netherlands East Indies where we would conducted Black Cat night reconnaissance missions. It was our home base for a while. At Moratai, we were all living in tents. Things were a little crude. Moratai is a small island south of the Philippines in the

Netherlands East Indies Group, and all operations were conducted off the water—working the liberation of the Philippines.

We were issued China-Burma patches to put on our jackets. Trouble was, it was normally too hot to wear jackets. Therefore, we didn't do it.

We've had a couple of eventful flights.

Late November, we searched for enemy shipping at sea and Mindanao, Sulu Archipelago, Borneo, and Celebes harbors.

On the 26th, we were in a night flight that lasted fourteen hours. We bombed, strafed, and sank a medium-sized enemy freighter-transport (Fox Tare Charlie) west of Jolo Island in the Sulu Archipelago.

Using land cover to his advantage, Lt. Turner made two direct hits with 250lb bombs. With a strafing run, we hit the vessel with the four fifty caliber wing guns, and twin thirties.

The target was seen to blow up and when the plane circled around for further observation, it had disappeared. Anti-aircraft fire from shore gun positions, and one on the ship was received during the attack.

A couple of weeks later on December 6th, we had a night flight that ended up lasting about fifteen hours. Cmdr. Gillette led a flight of three planes on a mission to attack shipping in the harbor at Balikpapan, Borneo.

In spite of unfavorable weather, all three planes reached the Borneo coast in the vicinity of Balikpapan, but were unable to complete the attack because of weather conditions.

Lt. Turner was negotiating a mountain pass in the Celebes under instrument conditions when we felt he starboard wing strike a hard, yielding object. The hit threw the plane into a left down wing position.

Lt. Turner asked me to get on the RADAR, which was fired up but on standby. Putting the plane into a steep climb, we kept up a running conversation until I started seeing a clear signal under the noise pattern.

I told him he could level off, which he did. At this point, the plane had a slight vibration so we continued on with our mission.

After returning to base, we found under examination the plane revealed a damaged wingtip float, a starboard running light, as well as, two deep indentations in the leading edge of the starboard wing well outboard, and several rips on the underside.

Several sizable wood fragments were found wedged in the edge of the wing and wing tip float. We concluded that we must've hit the top of the trees on the side of the mountain.

We continued with long range Cat anti-shipping patrols.

A few days after the incident with the trees, on Dec. 9th, we had a shorter hop (about 9.8 hours). We were searching for Lt. (jg) Shelley's plane which failed to return from patrol. Shelley Lt. (jg), Auburn AOMB2c, and Art Breslin ARM 2c, who was from Providence, were both killed in the crash. The rest of the crew was reported to be in the hands of friendly guerrillas.

We had another memorable night flight on December 11th. (12.5 hours). Sandakan Borneo, we bombed and strafed shipping, the docks, and barracks. Of the six 250lbs G.P. (general purpose) bombs dropped, one was seen to hit and sink a lugger, and two direct hits were made on the docks.

A second lugger was sunk by strafing.

During the entire stay at Moratai, the base was under constant night air attacks. Most of Moratai was controlled by the enemy. Patrols attacked the perimeter with some infiltration by small groups, the danger of the enemy breaking through the perimeter line was worrisome.

Black Cat patrols from Moratai were discontinued in mid-December. On the 28th, we left Moratai and arrived in Owi for some much needed R &R.

VPB 71

1945

The first few months of 1945 had been just as busy as the last few months of '44.

January 4, 1945: Moratai to USS Tangier AV-8 at Leyte Gulf, Luzon, Philippines. We were living aboard ship.

January 6: We had night flights. We were in the air about fifteen hours. We were covering a large convoy which was moving from Leyte to Lingayen Gulf, protecting them from possible enemy submarine contacts and bogeys.

Since we were Black Cats, we had to keep moving so the enemy couldn't find us. By January 12th, we were living aboard USS Barataria AVP-33 which is a small sea plane tender. Our new flights were now targeting the west coast of Formosa (Taiwan), and the China coast with offensive reconnaissance missions.

The Cats offensive attacks increased. At first the area wasn't being heavily protected by the Japs—unescorted merchant ships, leaving landing lights on at their Formosa seaplane base, etc. That luck didn't last. The Japs started increasing their shore searchlights and their anti-aircraft batteries increased, along with a more stringent escort of their merchant ships.

On January 22nd, a 12.8 hour night flight, we bombed the heavily fortified Mako Island, Pescadores.

We'd made a single run at low altitude and put four 250lb G.P bombs, and two 100lb incendiary clusters squarely on the barracks, shops, and warehouses. There was no return fire. The initial blows from the bombs were followed by a series of explosions and large fires.

We had another long night flight (13.1hrs) on January 29th. At Ishigaki Harbor in the Sakashima group, we sighted an old type Jap destroyer and two DE's.

As we were making our bombing run toward the three Jap ships, we had to break off. The attempted to hit us with light and medium anti-aircraft.

Weather tended to be a major hurtle for the Cats crews. Winds could go up to fifty knots, turbulence, and poor visibility all held possible cataclysmic difficulties for the crews on long range night missions into enemy territory.

We were flying on the west coast of Formosa, near Tainan, when a small Jap freighter was sighted (Sugar Charlie). Due to bad weather we had to make RADAR approaches. Taking over the RADAR, we made three approaches before we made visual contact.

Once we had visual, we dropped two 500lb bombs. This was also a 12.8 hour night flight. (February 1st) Making another run on RADAR, we then dropped our other two 500lb bombs. After that, we came back for a strafing run.

By this time, the ship had already taken water. We continued to search with RADAR, and failed to re-establish any contact with the vessel.

The next day was a bit rough on all of us—a heavy loss.

It was a Black Cats crew—crew 14: Lt. (jg) Albert John Lehmicke, Jr. and crew 14 (Charles H. White ACOM) went out on a mission but never returned. Searches for the missing plane came up empty-handed.

A few days later, a few of the crewmen were found on an island.

I flew with them in VP 71.

Early February, we were covering the west coast of Formosa when we spotted a Sugar Charlie (small freighter). The weather was fighting us and we had to make a couple of approaches using RADAR before we could get visual. By then the ship had heard us and took evasive maneuvers.

We dropped two 500lb bombs. Both missed the ship but one of them had landed close enough to the stern to stop it dead in the water.

A second run on the Jap ship was intended for the starboard, but due to visibility and high winds, we ended up across the beam of the target. The two 500lb bombs straddled the ship and enveloped the aft section in a geyser of water.

Lt. Turner made a tight turn and started another strafing run. The restricted visual was enough for us to see the Jap freighter sinking by the stern with her deck under water.

We used illumination by the plane's tracers and saw Japs abandoning ship. Circling back again, we failed to contact the ship by RADAR, nor had visual sighting.

More night flights kept us searching the coast. On February 16th, a 12.8 hour flight, we were patrolling along the west coast of Formosa, I made RADAR contact—three blips on the radar screen.

Visibility was very poor and we made multiple runs before we could make visual contact. Lt. Turner concentrated most of his effort on a Tare Baker class (the larger transport ship) and two small freighters near Takao, Formosa.

The Tare Baker was motionless in the water and down slightly by the stern. The two Sugar Charlies (small freighters) were strafed with 300 rounds while we were approaching the larger freighter.

After several runs, a direct hit was made with the 100lb bomb, and a fire was started in the forward hold of the ship.

We did four more runs with fifteen RADAR approaches between each drop. We spent over three hours making multiple runs with RADAR before we could get visual, expending all our bombs and ammo before we left the area.

February 20: Night Flight, 13 hours. We changed our search pattern around this time to include the China coast. We made a search of Amoy Harbor, Negat. On our return to base, we bombed a RADAR Station on the southern tip of Formosa.

On February 22nd, we landed at Clark Field, and had a chance to have a two-day liberty in Manila, Philippines.

Back to work on February 24th for another 12.5 hour night flight on the China coast of Swatow, Negat.

This was one of those really dark nights—a serious advantage for us since our plane was painted a flat black. I don't know if I said this or not, but depending on the night depends on how we fly. If there were clouds, we used the clouds for cover. The enemy couldn't spot us.

If there weren't any clouds to use for cover, we had to fly low. The enemy, if —when they heard us, was looking up and missed us. We had the element of surprise.

This particular night stands out for me. I had picked up blip on RADAR and had Lt. Turner make a run but just before release he made out a lighthouse.

That was too close for comfort!

On the return, we bombed the barracks at

Pescadores.

Another night flight (twelve hours) on February 28th, we patrolled the China Coast, Swataw to Amoy Harbor, and then over to Pescadores.

The harbor at Swataw was empty so we headed toward Amoy, which also had no sightings of ships. There were two unidentified aircraft, one seen visually, and one by RADAR. We attempted to search the inner harbor but were held off by anti-aircraft fire from the shore batteries.

We then headed for the Pescadores where we spotted several merchant ships and small craft. Observing the ships in the Mako harbor, Lt. Turner was flying low at 150 feet. We were making a glide bombing run on a Sugar Baker (large freighter) when we encountered return fire.

We dropped two 500lb bombs and one 250lb bomb. With the intense fire that resulted from the drops, we couldn't see if we'd made a hit.

With the release of the bombs, we were flying over the center of a circle of anti-aircraft positions. Shore batteries responded to our attack with anti-aircraft fire. Multiple hits were made on the Cat with most of the hits toward the front of the plane.

Two 20mm shells exploded in the cockpit, one through the bow, exploding behind the instrument panel—causing a fire. The other came directly below and exploded against the rudder bar on the port side of the plane directly under Lt. Turner's feet.

Another 20mm shell hit the port side in the navigation compartment. hitting the IFF equipment and causing the destructors to detonate.

Two men had serious injuries, Chief Smith, who was using the bow twin thirties was hit in the leg with a 20mm explosive shell, and PC Reardon, at his station in the tower, was also hit in the leg by shrapnel.

Taking immediate evasive maneuvers, as we were pulling out of our run, Lt. Turner dropped the rest of our bombs on unidentified buildings near the waterfront.

On the trip back to the base, I was acting as radioman, doing double-duty, sending messages, and also working the RADAR. On the RADAR, we had a bogie following us for a while, but he didn't fire.

Blencoe and Barrett administered first aid on the injured men.

When we returned to Lingayen Gulf, we beached our aircraft and got the men aboard the ship. Chief Smith lost part of his leg.

We realized how lucky we were when, later, they counted 65 holes in the hull. Major structural repairs were needed to the hull, rewiring the electrical system, and we'd have to replace more than half of the cockpit instruments. But, both engines were fine.

20 mm hits had made 6 to 10 inch holes, causing structural damage in the starboard wheel well, after-step keel, and the leading edge center section of the wing.

At the beginning of March, 1945, we started living at Jinamoc Island. Making a few patrols from Jinamoc, we had no enemy contacts.

We also made several small hops to Samar, Tacloban. It's in the eastern Visayas region of the Philippines.

Liberty! Clark Field, liberty in Manila, Nichols Field.

We had to make some repairs to the plane and on March 29th we had a test flight.

We're back in commission.

A few days later on the 31st, we moved to Samar

Island. We did a patrol from Samar tracking a typhoon approaching the Philippine area.

April, May, and June: We're pretty much doing the same old stuff, typical all day hops averaging about 13 hours, doing Dumbo runs, patrols, reconnaissance missions, searches for missing aircraft, courier missions, etc.

In May, we carried a reconnaissance group from Leyte to Mindanao, where they met with guerilla leaders. A few days later, we were called out to search for an Army transport plane (C-46). It had been seen to crash in the water. Circling the area, there were crash boats standing by and we weren't needed, so we returned to base. Unfortunately, no one survived the crash.

We made a patrol covering an English DD which had been hit. We've covered a couple of army strikes; one at Suluan Point, and also at Negros.

On June 14th I was discharged from VPB 71 and would be heading home. When I returned from leave, they would give me my orders.

It was a long and interesting trip.

First it would be from Samar to Guam R5D—then from Guam to Kwajalein; Kwajalein to Johnson and Johnson to Kaneohe Air Station, Hawaii.

I left for the States on June 22, 1945 aboard the USS General R.E.Callen (AP139). I arrived at Naval Air Station Alameda, California on June 28[th,] and was heading to Rhode Island for a thirty day leave.

I was going home!

I arrived back to the West Coast after being home on leave for thirty days. I was assigned to duty station in Alameda.

The war's over!

I will thank Colonel Paul Tibbets, his Enola Gay, and celebrate August 14th for the rest of my life.

I had the chance to get out on points received.

I think, at this time, I realized that it was enough.

I Was Just a Radioman is about the true life WW2 experiences, memoirs, of Chief ARM Henry P. Lawrence—a Pearl Harbor survivor, Black Cat, and decorated war veteran.

Chief ARM Henry P. Lawrence was awarded the Distinguished Flying Cross, three Air Medals, the Navy Unit Citation, the Philippine Liberation Medal, and Air Crew wings with three stars. He was authorized a total of seven stars on his Asian Pacific Ribbon. He returned home in 1945 as Chief ARM. He was also recommended for the Silver Star, but that was not awarded.

After the war, Henry P. Lawrence spent another eighteen years in the Navy Reserves, leaving the service as a Master Chief Petty Officer.

Paul Tibbets, Pilot
6 AUG. 1945

ENOLA GAY

882

12-4-99

FOREWORD

It is unfortunate that the idea of a War History was not inaugurated until 1944, well past the turning point of the War. Better that it was conceived in 1944 however, than not at all. For by virtue of the War Histories of all Naval units, a permanent record which cannot be distorted by time, will be available to all students of Naval Warfare; to all who, by no choice of their own, saw only one small corner of this global war; and to all who, finding their memories growing dim, can turn to the War History to help them re-live the most vital years of their own and the world's existence.

For Patrol Bombing Squadron SEVENTY-ONE, however, the War History does little injustice. For it was the re-forming of the squadron in 1944 that saw SEVENTY-ONE start on her truly eventful days. The preceding years, although full of service, are well covered by the summary of pre-1944 activities.

And so in April 1944, this War History takes up the story of a cross-sectional group of young American Naval fliers and aircrewmen, gathered together to train, and somewhat to their surprise, to fight, in PBY-5A's - Catalinas - a plane originally designed for patrol and rescue work, but now called upon to attack heavily armed enemy units at the closest possible range — the Black Cats!

N. C. GILLETTE, Jr.,
Commander, U. S. Navy,
Commanding Officer.

1 May 1945

DR Form 3
Box. N. Y. 5-28-40
Orig. & 5—1000 Sets

Headquarters of the
Commandant First Naval District
Building 39, Navy Yard, Boston, Mass.

July 16, 1940.

From: Commandant First Naval District.

To: LAWRENCE, Henry Paul AS 0-1 400 73 87 USNR.

SUBJECT: ORDERS to training duty with pay — ENLISTED MAN.

1. In accordance with the provisions of law, requiring the annual performance of training duty by officers and men of the Organized Reserve, you will report to the Medical Officer **Ninth Division** Newport, R. I. on or before July 27, 1940, for physical examination.

2. If you are found not physically qualified, paragraphs 3, 4, 5 and 6 of these orders will be considered canceled, and you will return to your home.

3. If found physically qualified, you will report to the Commanding Officer, of the **9th** Division at Newport, R. I. for training duty for a period of fourteen days on the U.S.S. WILLIAMS in duties appropriate to your rating and class.

4. Upon completion of this training duty, you will be examined physically. Upon return to your home, you will consider yourself released from training duty. One copy of these orders with all endorsements will be forwarded to the Bureau of Navigation and one copy to the Commandant upon completion of training.

5. Bring these orders with you upon reporting for training duty. Inability to comply with these orders must be reported to your Commanding Officer immediately.

6. You are entitled to active duty pay of your rating during the fourteen days training duty and for the time required in traveling (by shortest usually traveled route) from your home to the place of reporting and from place of detachment to your home upon completion of training duty.

7. The above named enlisted man is not drawing a pension, disability allowance, disability compensation, or retired pay from the Government of the United States, nor has he a claim pending therefor covering the period of these orders.

John H. Keefe,
(John H. Keefe, Comdr., U. S. N. (Ret.)
By direction.

ACTION	PLACE	TIME	DATE	SIGNATURE
Received	Newport, Rhode Island	2000	7-17-40	Henery Paul Lawrence Reservist
Left Home	Newport, Rhode Island	0700	7-27-40	Henery Paul Lawrence Reservist
Phys. Qual. for training	Newport, Rhode Island	2000	7-24-40	Chas. H. M. Stoops Med. Off.
Reported on board USS WILLIAMS	Newport, R. I.	0900	7-27/40	H. Myers, Lt., USN Off.
Phys. Exam. For Release	USS WILLIAMS	0800	8/9/40	H. M. Stoops,CDR (MC)MC
Detached, USS WILLIAMS Duty Completed	Newport, R. I.	0900	8/9/40	H. Myers, Lt., USN Off.
Proceeded	Newport, R. I.	1000	8/9/40	Henry Paul Lawrence Reservist
Arrived Home	Newport, R. I.	1100	8/9/40	Henry Paul Lawrence Reservist

Distribution of completed copies—Orig. and 4 copies with all end. to Dish. Off.
  1 Bu.Nav.
  1 Bu.S&A (Ret. Pay Div.)
  1 District files
  1 C.O.

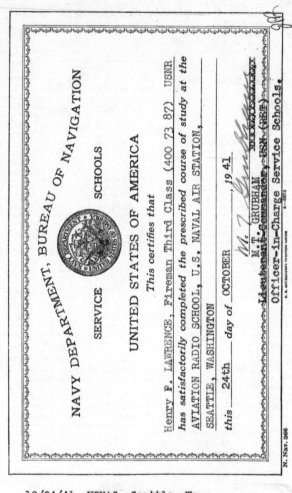

NAVY DEPARTMENT, BUREAU OF NAVIGATION

SERVICE SCHOOLS

UNITED STATES OF AMERICA

This certifies that

Henry F. LAWRENCE, Fireman Third Class (400 73 87) USNR
has satisfactorily completed the prescribed course of study at the
AVIATION RADIO SCHOOL, U.S. NAVAL AIR STATION,
SEATTLE, WASHINGTON

this ___24th___ *day of* OCTOBER _____, 19 41

M. T. Grubham

M.T. GRUBHAM
Lieutenant Commander, USN (RET)
Officer—in—Charge Service Schools.

N. Nav. 366

10/24/41 USNAS, Seattle, Wn.
It is certified that all entries
on the face of this report are
correct.

J.P. RICHARDSON
CRE USN (RET)
OFFICER IN CHARGE
AV. RADIO SCHOOL

NAVY MOTHERS HONORED AT ARMISTICE DAY EXERCISES

These eight women, with four or more sons each in service, were given gold pins by Mayor Herbert E. Macauley Wednesday. They include Mrs. Eva G. Brawner, Mrs. Lucy M. Spaulding, Mrs. Lurza Furtado, Mrs. Mary S. Lawrence, Mrs. Kathleen Ostroski, Mrs. Marie Viti, Mrs. Daisy Beattie and Mrs. Caroline Wardlow.
—Kerschner Photo

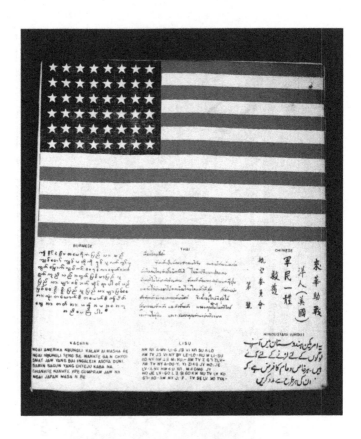

American Flag with Pacific
Area Languages

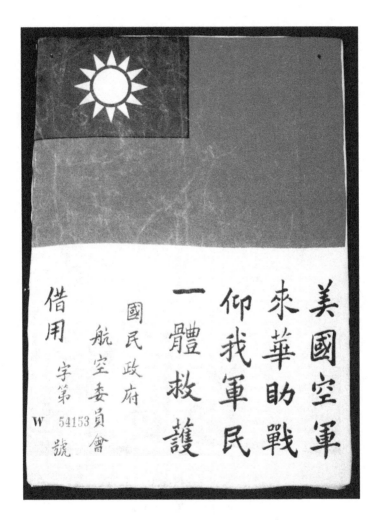

美國空軍
來華助戰
仰我軍民
一體救護

國民政府
航空委員會

借用
字第
W 54153
號

Chinese Flag WW II

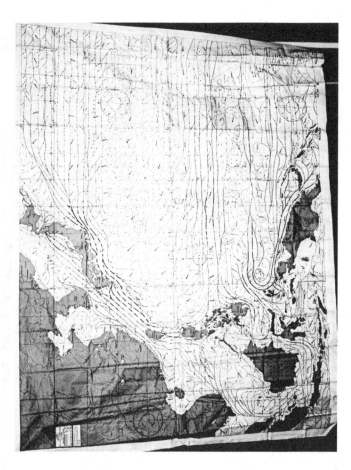

Silk Survival Map
Pacific Ocean

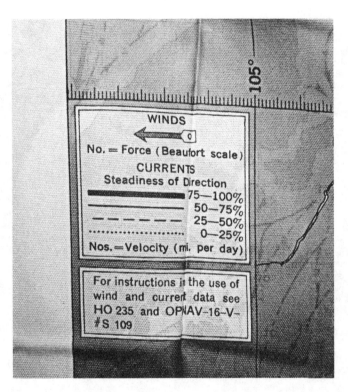

105°

WINDS

No. = Force (Beaufort scale)

CURRENTS
Steadiness of Direction

75—100%
50—75%
25—50%
0—25%

Nos. = Velocity (mi. per day)

For instructions in the use of wind and current data see HO 235 and OPNAV–16–V–#S 109

Silk Survival Map Inset

Insigna Designed by
Milton Caniff

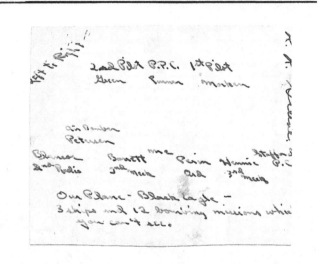

The Black Eagle Crew

Black Cat Stamp VPB 71

F39/(02-kd)

Serial: 1233   31 December 1944

From: The Commander, Fleet Air Wing SEVENTEEN.
To   :   The Commanding Officer, Patrol Bombing Squadron 71.

Subject: Display of Insignia in Recognition of Destruction
           to Enemy Surface Vessel.

Reference: (a) CinCPacFlt Ltr. 511-44 dated 28 Sept. 1944.

    1.   In recognition of sinking one Japanese PTC,
06-00 N 121-40 E, on 27 November by crew number 8, you are
hereby authorized to paint the prescribed insignia on your
assigned aircraft, or its replacement, while in the squadron.

    2.   Crew:

             Lieut. A.O. TURNER
             Lieut.(jg) C.L. MONKEN
             Ensign R.R. GREENE

             PETERSEN, H.J.   ACM2c
             BLESCOE, H.A.   AMM3c
             LAWRENCE, H.P.   ARM1c
             REARDON, L.E.   AMM2c
             BARRETT, G.A.   AMM3c
             PERIN, R.E.   AOM1c

                                    G. B. JONES

Copy to:
    VPB-71 Bulletin Board

P15(F-0-50/28)

Serial: 246   22 September 1945

From: Commander Seventh Fleet.
To :   Commander Aircraft, Philippine Sea Frontier.

Subject: Recommendations for Awards.

Reference: (a) ComAir7thFlt conf 2nd end ser 01497 of 20 aug 45.

1.   You are advised that reference (a) has been presented
to and considered by the Seventh Fleet Board of Awards. After careful
consideration the Board was of the opinion that the services preformed
by:

        LIEUTENANT (JG) ROBERT K. ANDERSON, U.S. NAVAL RESERVE
        LIEUTENANT (JG) WILLIAM A. DE HAAN, U.S. NAVAL RESERVE
        LIEUTENANT (JG) ROBERT R. GARRARD, U.S. NAVAL RESERVE
        LIEUTENANT (JG) CARL W. MAYNARD, U.S. NAVAL RESERVE
        LIEUTENANT (JG) CLIFFORD L. MORKEN, U.S. NAVAL RESERVE
        LIEUTENANT (JG) ROBERT L. POTTER, U.S. NAVAL RESERVE

        COX, Charles R., Aviation Chief Radioman, U.S.N.
        FEIGHT, Louis M., Aviation Chief Metalsmith, U.S.N.
        GRAY, James A., Aviation Chief Machinist's Mate, U.S.N.
        LAWRENCE, Henry F., Aviation Chief Radioman, U.S.N.R.
        PERIN, Warren W., Aviation Chief Ordnanceman, U.S.N.R.
        PETERSEN, Henrik J., Aviation Ordnanceman First Class, U.S.N.R.
        STAFFORD, Carl, Jr., Aviation Machinist's Mate First Class, U.S.N.R.
        WILANDER, Walter C., Aviation Radioman First Class, U.S.N.R.
        BARRETT, Gordon A., Aviation Machinist's Mate Second Class, U.S.N.R.
        BLENCOE, Harry A., Jr., Aviation Radioman Second Class, U.S.N.
        HOLMER, Robert A., Aviation Ordnanceman Second Class, U.S.N.R.
        JACOBSEN, Odd A., Aviation Radioman Second Class, U.S.N.R.
        FLOFFERT, William L., Aviation Ordnanceman Second Class, U.S.N.
        SCOTT, Ernest L., Aviation Machinist's Mate Second Class, U.S.N.R.
        NEDEAU, Laurence E., Aviation Machinist's Mate Third Class, U.S.N.R.

during the periods set out in reference (a), while meritorious, did not merit
special recognition, and recommended that no action be taken toward awards in
these cases.

2.   The recommendations of the Board of Awards have been approved
by the Commander Seventh Fleet.

                                THOS. S. COMBS
                                CHIEF OF STAFF

February 1932

Date	Type of Machine	Number of Machine	Duration of Flight	Character of Flight	Pilot	Passengers	REMARKS
20	08XX	48517	13.0		Lt. Turner		Night "Recon" China coast. / Amoy Hbr.—Bombed Godan / Stilson South tip of Formosa
22	"	4639	2.0		"		Ship to Strip – Night recon / Turn over Manila – Landed / at Clark Field – Refueled —
24	"	4639	.4		"		Ship to Strip
24	"	"	12.5		"		Night "Recon" – China coast – / Swatow – Nearly hit lighthouse / that we were homing in on / off China coast – Spotted what / junk – Bombed Parachút / Parachees
25	"	"	12.0		"		Night "Recon" – Foochean / China coast – Swatow – Amoy / Hbr. Over to Pescadores / badly shot up while making / run on E.Brelin in Hbr. / Chief Smith badly wounded / finally had to set off all of

Total time to date.

18 November 1957

From: _____
    (Name) LAWRENCE Henry Paul (Serv. No.) (Rate) (Branch)
To: Chief of Naval Personnel (Attn:)
Via: Commanding Officer, Naval Reserve Surface Division 1-35(M)

Subj: Campaign and service medals; request for

Ref: (a) Navy and Marine Corps Awards Manual (Part IV) (NavPers 15,790)

1. In accordance with the provisions of reference (a), it is requested that the following checked (X) medals, if entitled thereto, be forwarded to me at the above address:

World War II Victory Medal   X

American Defense Service Medal   X

American Area Campaign Medal   X

European-African-Middle Eastern Area Campaign Medal   _____

Asiatic-Pacific Area Campaign Medal   _____

Korean Service Medal   _____

National Defense Service Medal   _____

Navy Occupation Service Medal   _____

China Service Medal   _____

Henry Paul Lawrence
(Signature)

USNR SURFACE DIVISION 1-35(M)
USNRTC, NEWPORT, RHODE ISLAND

18 November 1957
(Date)

FIRST ENDORSEMENT

From: Commanding Officer
To: Chief of Naval Personnel (Attn:)

1. Forwarded, recommending approval.

H. E. TUTTLE, JR.

HENRY P. LAWRENCE
GETS FLYING CROSS

Chief Radioman Cited for Aerial Flight During Operations Against Japs

Henry P. Lawrence, aviation chief radioman, U. S. N.R., son of Mr. and Mrs. Anthony C. Lawrence of 18 Dearborn street, has received the Distinguished Flying Cross for achievement in aerial flight during operations in the Southwestern Pacific, First Naval District headquarters in Boston has announced

The citation accompanying the award to Lawrence, who has been in the service five years, and signed by Secretary of the Navy James V. Forrestal, acting in behalf of President Truman, states the Newporter earned the decoration for heroism and extraordinary achievement in aerial flight as an air-crewman during operations against Japanese forces from December 18, 1944, to February 1, 1945. Participating in 20 combat missions over hostile territory in the vicinity of enemy operational airfields, the citation continues, Lawrence rendered valuable service to his pilot, thereby contributing to the success of his plane.

Henry P. Lawrence
(on the right)
Receiving the Distinguished
Navy Cross

Made in the USA
Las Vegas, NV
21 September 2023

77899388R00049